IT'S YOUR LEAR

LEAD

BRIAN SENIOR
Foreword by BOBBY WOLFF

HOW TO PLAY BRIDGE

B T BATSFORD

First published 1998
© Brian Senior 1998

ISBN 0 7134 8258 3

A CIP catalogue record for this book is available
from the British Library.

Typeset by Apsbridge Services Ltd, Nottingham.

Printed in Singapore
for the publishers,
B. T. Batsford Ltd, 583 Fulham Road,
London SW6 5BY

A BATSFORD BRIDGE BOOK
Series Editor: Tony Sowter
Commissioning Editor: Paul Lamford

contents

foreword

Bridge is a game enjoyed by many millions of players all over the world.

In these days of rising commercial pressures, increasing leisure and greater longevity, bridge has the potential to break down social and ethnic barriers and to keep the wheels of the brain turning in both the old and the young. Apart from that, bridge at whatever level is a very inexpensive game; all you need to play is a flat surface that the four players can sit round with a pack of cards and, of course, an understanding as to how to play the game.

It is for these reasons that I am particularly pleased to welcome the 'How to Play Bridge' series which has been specially designed to make the game easy to follow for beginners, no matter what their age. I believe that you will find the whole series well presented and particularly easy to read.

I believe that after studying the 'How to Play Bridge' series you will not only be off to a good start, you will be totally enthralled by this great game.

Bobby Wolff
Dallas, Texas
March 1997

introduction

It is a fact that defense is the most difficult of the three main areas of the game of bridge and, without question, the most difficult single play by the defense is the first one, the opening lead. It is also the single most important card played on any bridge deal, often deciding the final success or failure of the contract.

Why is the opening lead so difficult? After the opening lead has been made, the dummy goes down and this gives the other three players extra information on which to base their strategies. The player on opening lead has only the sight of his own thirteen cards, plus what clues may be gleaned from the bidding, to guide him.

The choice of opening lead can be broken up into two stages. These are which suit to lead and, having decided that, which card from within that suit. The first is a matter of judgement, the second largely a question of systemic agreement – just as is, for example, the strength of your partnership's one no trump opening bid.

As it is the simpler part of the process and gives us a firm base from which to work, we should start by considering the question 'which card?'

which card?

An important consideration to bear in mind is that declarer has an enormous advantage over the poor defenders. Because he can see his partner's hand (dummy) he knows his side's combined assets and can plan how best to utilise them. Each defender sees his own hand, plus the dummy, but not partner's, making the planning much harder.

One way in which the defenders can try to overcome declarer's advantage is by trying to tell each other as much as they can about their hands. No, not by smiling and nodding when they like the suit led and frowning to express dislike. That would be most unfair. What I mean is that they can pass messages by the actual cards they play.

Suppose that you decided to lead a suit in which you held the king, the queen and the jack, and you simply played the card nearest to your thumb. Partner would know that you had some good cards in the suit but, apart from the one actually led, how could he tell which good cards?

Now, suppose that instead of leading the card next to your thumb you always led the same card from the same holding. Would partner not now have more information about your hand?

Suppose, for example, that you always led the top card in a sequence of touching honor cards – the king from KQJ, queen from QJ10, and so on. If you agree this in advance then, for example, if you lead a queen partner immediately knows that you probably also hold the jack and maybe the ten but cannot hold the king; if you lead the jack you will normally have the ten but cannot hold the queen.

That is what actually happens. Other agreements are possible and some expert pairs prefer different ways of doing things, but the standard arrangement is exactly that: to lead the top card from a sequence of touching honors.

It makes sense to lead one of the honors when holding a sequence, of course. Suppose that your holding in a suit is KQJ2. If you lead the two you may allow declarer to win a cheap trick with the ten. Lead one of your honors, and either you win the trick or you force out declarer's ace and now your other two honors are established as winners for when you regain the lead.

Suppose that you hold a broken sequence such as KJ10 or Q109. You ignore the top card and look at the cards that are actually touching. The standard lead from the above holdings is the jack and the ten respectively. In each case you lead the top card from the actual sequence. The technical name for these broken sequences is an interior sequence.

Why lead an honor from an interior sequence? Again, you want to avoid giving declarer a cheap trick. Imagine that a suit is distributed around the table like this:

♠ J54

♠ Q1092 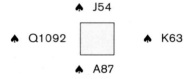 ♠ K63

♠ A87

If you lead the two declarer can play small from the dummy and your partner will be left with an unappetising choice. If he plays low declarer wins a cheap trick with the seven; if he rises with the king declarer wins with the ace and can later lead up towards dummy's jack and you cannot prevent him from eventually making a second trick in the suit.

Now suppose that you lead the ten, top of your sequence, on the first round of the suit. If declarer plays dummy's jack partner beats it with the king.

Declarer can take the ace but both your queen and nine are now established as winners. And if declarer chooses to play low from dummy on the first round, why, partner also plays low, retaining his king to beat the jack on a later trick. Declarer can take the ace whenever he likes but he will no longer score an extra trick with the jack.

When you hold a long suit which does not contain an honor sequence, you should lead a small card. So KJ754, though it is a suit containing two honor cards, does not include a sequence and you would not lead one of the honors. In fact, the standard lead from a long suit headed by one or more honors but no sequence is the fourth highest card, in the above example, the five. We will look at why the fourth card is chosen later.

Beginners often want to lead out their highest cards and would start with the king from the aforementioned holding. What they have to get used to is that defense is a team game. It doesn't matter which defender wins a trick, they still count the same for the partnership.

Say that you do lead the king from KJ754. If declarer has both the ace and queen between his hand and dummy he will normally make them both and your king will be dead. Equally, had you chosen to lead a small card, declarer could have won the queen and still had the ace for later. So the end result will be the same either way.
But imagine that partner holds one of the missing high cards. If you lead a small card he will play it. His queen will do just as good a job of forcing declarer's ace as would have your king. Again, the end result will be much the same whichever lead you make.

But now consider a layout like this one:

♠ 762

♠ KJ754   ♠ A9

♠ Q108

Lead the king and you will win the trick. You can lead a second round of the suit to partner's ace and that is two tricks for your side. But declarer will have played the eight and the ten on those two tricks and will have the queen left to win a trick himself.

Now try it again if you lead a small card to the first trick. Partner wins the ace and returns the nine − and whether declarer chooses to play the ten or

the queen doesn't matter. You beat the ten
with the jack, the queen with the king,
and your side makes all the tricks in
the suit, declarer gets nothing. By
leading a small card you made it
possible to trap declarer's
high cards.

From a doubleton, a holding of
precisely two cards in a suit, the
standard lead is the higher card,
irrespective of whether either or both are
honors.

Finally, if you choose to lead from a suit containing
three or more small cards but no honor, the
traditional lead was the top card, 'Top of Nothing'.
Experience has shown, however, that to lead the
nine from 9643, say, occasionally costs a trick.
Accordingly, the more modern approach is to
always lead the second highest card, the six from
9643, the eight from 982, and so on.

recommended leads

There are some variations in the recommended
lead according to whether the contract is in no
trumps or in a suit. We will look at the reasons for
these variations later. For now, here is a table of
the standard leads from various suit holdings.

Holding	Against NT	In a Suit Contract
AK	K	K
AK4	K	A
AKJ103	A	A
KQJ	K	K
QJ10	Q	Q
J109	J	J
1098	10	10
AQJ	Q	A
KJ10	J	J
Q1092	10	10
J108	J	J
J103	J	J
J1032	2	J/2
A7532	3	A
A73	3	A
A3	A	A
AJ109	J	A
A1095	10	A
K7	K	K
K73	3	3
K732	2	2
K8732	3	3
K106432	4	4
Q75	5	5
J864	4	4
107532	3	3
73	7	7
863	6	6
8742	7	7
87653	7	7

leads against no trump contracts

The first thing to consider before selecting your opening lead is 'What am I trying to achieve?' The answer is very simple – you are trying to defeat your opponents' contract. The level of the contract tells you how many tricks declarer needs if he is to fulfill his contract.

Say he is playing in 3NT. To make his contract declarer must make at least nine tricks. Therefore, your goal is to take at least five tricks. As there are only thirteen tricks in total to be shared out between declarer and the defenders, if you take five it is impossible for declarer to take nine.

The second thing which should never be lost sight of is that it doesn't matter which defender wins the tricks, they are playing as a team. All that matters is that between them they win enough tricks to prevent declarer from making his contract. Accordingly, as the defense unfolds it will often be appropriate for one defender to sacrifice his high cards in the common good, perhaps promoting winners for his partner.

Let's see what this means to the choice of opening lead. Say your opponents bid 1NT – 3NT and you are on lead holding:

♠ KQJ10
♥ AK2
♦ 432
♣ 432

What should you choose? Many beginners would start by cashing the two sure heart winners and then switch to a spade. But suppose that this is the full lay-out:

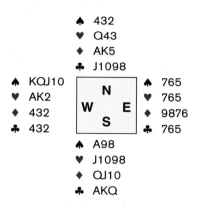

```
            ♠  432
            ♥  Q43
            ♦  AK5
            ♣  J1098
♠  KQJ10   ┌──────────┐  ♠  765
♥  AK2     │    N     │  ♥  765
♦  432     │ W     E  │  ♦  9876
♣  432     │    S     │  ♣  765
            └──────────┘
            ♠  A98
            ♥  J1098
            ♦  QJ10
            ♣  AKQ
```

If you cash the ace and king of hearts then play a spade, declarer can win the spade and has ten tricks to cash – the spade, two hearts, three diamonds and four clubs.

Now suppose that you lead spades until declarer takes the ace, but without releasing the ace and king of hearts. Without a heart trick declarer has only eight winners and cannot fulfill his contract. So, sooner or later, he must lead a heart and now you can win and cash the remainder of your spades plus the other heart winner. This time you get five tricks, two hearts and three spades, and the contract is defeated.

The message is to take a long-term view. Rather than rushing to grab your winners at the start, hang on to them until you have established the number you need to defeat the contract. On the above hand the ace and king of hearts gave you control of the heart suit, preventing declarer from taking any tricks there until he had knocked them both out. If you cashed the hearts at the start, what you were doing was declarer's work, establishing extra tricks for him; if, on the other hand, you started by attacking spades, you would be doing your side's work, establishing your extra tricks.

There are few absolute rules in bridge but a good general principle is to lead your long suits against no trump contracts, hoping to establish extra length tricks for the defense, rather than cashing your high cards at the beginning of the hand.

Against the same 3NT contract you have to lead from:

♠ Q9652
♥ A85
♦ 73
♣ 984

If you cash the ace of hearts you get one trick but then, unless by some fluke you have found partner with long strong hearts, you are no further forward towards your ultimate goal of taking at least five tricks. Far better is to lead a spade. Your hope is that if partner can help out with a high card or two in spades you might be able to establish several tricks in the suit, perhaps sufficient to defeat 3NT.

When you have an unsupported honor, as is the queen here, it is best to lead a small card instead. If partner cannot help out, the queen will achieve no more than the small card. But suppose this is the lay-out:

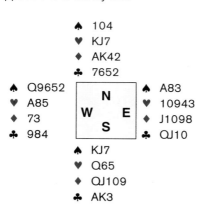

```
              ♠ 104
              ♥ KJ7
              ♦ AK42
              ♣ 7652
  ♠ Q9652      ┌─────────┐   ♠ A83
  ♥ A85        │    N    │   ♥ 10943
  ♦ 73         │  W   E  │   ♦ J1098
  ♣ 984        │    S    │   ♣ QJ10
               └─────────┘
              ♠ KJ7
              ♥ Q65
              ♦ QJ109
              ♣ AK3
```

If you lead the queen to the first trick, declarer can win the king and still has a second stopper in the suit, his jack and dummy's ten being equals against partner's ace. By playing on hearts, declarer will be able to establish two extra tricks and make his contract in some comfort.

But try leading a low spade to the first trick. Partner can win the ace and shoot a second one back through declarer's remaining king, jack. However declarer plays he gets only one trick and meanwhile you can establish your long cards and make four spade tricks in all plus the ace of hearts – one down!

By starting with a small card you made a less comital lead, allowing you to judge when it would be most beneficial to your side for the queen to be played.

Of course, the other side of the coin is that when it is your partner who leads a small card you must do the best you can to help him. Take this deal:

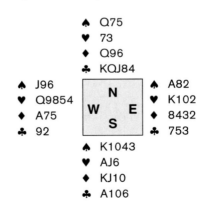

```
              ♠ Q75
              ♥ 73
              ♦ Q96
              ♣ KQJ84
♠ J96                        ♠ A82
♥ Q9854        N             ♥ K102
♦ A75       W     E          ♦ 8432
♣ 92           S             ♣ 753
              ♠ K1043
              ♥ AJ6
              ♦ KJ10
              ♣ A106
```

Say that West leads a low heart against South's 3NT contract. If East is too mean to sacrifice his king, preferring to save it in the hope of winning a trick with it later, what happens? East puts in the ten and declarer gets a cheap trick with the jack. He proceeds to play on diamonds, establishing two tricks there to go with five clubs and two hearts, and brings home his contract.

But East's play of the ♥10 at trick one gave declarer a trick to which he was not really entitled. Try it again with East doing his duty and nobly sacrificing his king for the greater good. Declarer can win or duck this trick but the defenders can always trap his jack by leading the next round of hearts from the East side, holding him to just the one heart trick. Say that declarer takes the first trick. Eventually, East gains the lead with his ♠A – declarer doesn't have nine tricks without playing on spades – and now the return of the ♥10 traps the ♥J and allows West to take the rest of the hearts.

So, a good general rule is to lead your longest suit against a no trump contract, unless the bidding has offered some clues to the contrary, and with two suits of equal length lead the stronger, on the basis that the stronger the suit the less help you will need from partner to establish tricks there. Your idea is that even if you don't win the opening trick, you will eventually set up long cards in the suit led as winners. Obviously, the longer the suit you lead, the more eventual winners you can hope to establish.

the rule of eleven

Having decided to lead a small card from a suit headed by a broken honor holding, does it matter which small card you choose?

The answer, as you may have already guessed, is yes, it does. If you consistently choose the same small card then partner can glean extra information from your opening lead.

The standard lead is the fourth highest card in the suit led. That means the four from K864; the five from AQ752, and so on.

On its own, consistently leading the fourth highest card can sometimes give partner some useful information. If, for example, you lead a two, it is immediately clear that you cannot have more than four cards in the suit as the two is the lowest card. Equally, if you lead any card and partner can see all the lower ones between his own hand and dummy then he knows you cannot hold more than four cards in the suit. But if you use something called The Rule of Eleven, you can also learn something about declarer's hand. Here is how it works:

Start with the magic number of eleven. Subtract the number of spots on the card partner leads. Next, see how many cards higher than the one led you can see in your own hand and in dummy. Subtract that number from the previous total and the figure remaining is the number of cards declarer holds which are higher than the one led. Sounds complicated? Let's look at an example of how it works.

Say that partner leads the six and you see K103 in dummy and AQ9 in your own hand.

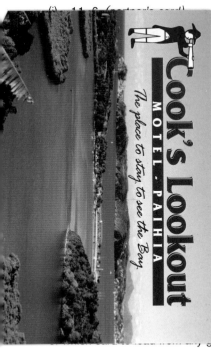

(i)   11 − 6 (partner's card)   =   5

                                        =   3

                                  six) =   0

than the six
as his fourth best
om a collection of
ly). If declarer
put in the nine. If
the six the nine
ut for the rule of
pted to play the
hance to win a
the next round of

e hang of the Rule,
at there is a benefit
nt in your choice
ven holding.

ace for unblock

There is one special honor lead which only applies in no trump contracts. Where normally you lead ace from ace, king against a suit contract, the conventional lead in no trump is the king. The ace is a special lead. Unless obviously not the case from the bidding and your own hand, if partner leads an ace the message is that his suit is a very good one, probably missing only one honor card. What he wants is to discover where that missing honor might be. If you hold the jack or queen, therefore, you should throw it under the ace. With no honor to unblock in this fashion you should signal your distribution, playing high-low with an even number of cards in the suit led, low-high with an odd number. This way, partner can work out how many cards declarer holds in the suit and whether the missing honor will fall if he cashes his king.

Say partner has led the ♠A from:

♠ AKJ108
♥ 764
♦ 85
♣ J84

Dummy turns up with three low spades.

If you play the queen it is easy for partner to cash the rest of the suit; if you play a small spade,

e.g. the two, partner will read you for an odd
number – hopefully three as if you have only a
singleton declarer always has the suit stopped –
and again partner can bash out the king and
expect to drop declarer's queen; if you play a
high spot card, such as the seven, partner
will read you for a doubleton and declarer
for queen to three. Now the queen is
not dropping and partner's only
chance will be to switch to another
suit, hoping that you can gain the
lead and return your remaining
spade, thereby trapping the queen.

Leading your longest and strongest suit is
a good general rule; however, as with any
rule, it is only a guide and should not be
followed blindly. Let's look at a few exceptions,
usually suggested by the bidding.
If your partner has bid a suit he will usually have
both length and strength there, particularly if he has
overcalled or opened with one of a major suit.
Unless you have a good alternative in your own
hand, it will usually be a good idea to lead partner's
suit. Remember that defense is a partnership thing.
What you want to lead is your partnership's
combined best suit, not just your own favorite.
When partner has bid a suit, that suit will frequently
be your side's best combined holding.

Say that South plays 3NT after your partner
opened 1♠ and you hold:

♠ 106
♥ Q9763
♦ 854
♣ 1097

You should lead the ♠10, top of a doubleton as usual. You know that partner holds at least five spades and, because he opened the bidding, he must have a fair number of high cards in his hand. Hopefully, he can get in often enough to establish and then cash his spades.

If you lead a heart, you need a lot of luck to make many heart tricks. Even if partner has some high card strength in hearts and can help you to establish your suit, how will you ever gain the lead to cash your winners?

The play often develops into a race to see which side can establish the required number of tricks first. While a heart lead on the above hand may not give a trick away in the heart suit, it could give declarer a vital tempo, putting him one step ahead in the race.

The time to consider leading your own suit even though partner has bid another one is when your own suit is long and strong, needing only a little help from partner to establish it, you have reason to think you will be able to gain the lead to cash your established tricks, and you have no help for partner if you lead his suit.

You hold:

♠ 7
♥ KJ1094
♦ A32
♣ 6432

and hear the auction:

West	North	East	South
Pass	1♣	1♠	2NT
Pass	3NT	All Pass	

It sounds as though declarer has partner's spades well covered and partner can hardly have sufficient strength to both establish and get in again to cash his suit when you have 8 HCP and the opponents have bid game. Better to lead a heart and hope to find partner with the ace or queen. In either case you will be able to establish your suit quickly and hope to get in with the ♦A to cash it.

Which heart should you lead? The jack is correct, the top card in the interior sequence.

Another time when you might consider an alternative to leading your longest suit is when the opposition have bid it, suggesting that the bidder will have length and/or strength there. To lead the suit may merely serve to give declarer a cheap trick.

There is a difference here between different situations in which the opponents bid your suit. If, for example, declarer has opened one of a major, promising five cards, there would be little point in leading from a holding such as Q8643. Partner can hardly have a holding which will allow you to get this suit going.

But, if declarer has opened 1♣ and rebid 1NT over his partner's 1♠ response, it is quite possible that he has opened a three card suit on, say, a 3-4-3-3 distribution. You should still be wary about leading declarer's suit, as he will still have genuine length and strength there more often than not, but the odds are quite a lot better.

Even when an opponent has shown a five card suit you can still lead it if your own holding is both long and strong. By all means lead a suit such as QJ1097. You will give declarer nothing he could not make for himself as you are leading from a solid sequence and if partner happens to hold the king you could do very well.

Where the bidding has discouraged you from leading your longest suit, try the effect of leading from a holding of three, or even two, small cards. If you are lucky you may hit partner's strength and even if you do not you will probably do no real harm.

The auction can give useful pointers in other ways. Say that your left hand opponent (LHO) opens 3♥ and 3NT is bid on your right, ending the auction. What does that auction tell you?

You should realise that dummy will hold a reasonable seven card heart suit but not a lot of outside strength. Nonetheless, that long suit may take very little establishing and provide declarer with a source of several quick tricks. What about leading from this hand against the above auction?

> ♠ J7632
> ♥ 85
> ♦ Q42
> ♣ KQ8

A low spade lead may eventually establish tricks for your side but they will come too late unless partner has at least two honors in spades. An attractive alternative would be to lead the ♣K, hoping to hit partner's long suit. Give partner as little as ♣Jxxxx and a heart stopper and you may defeat an otherwise impregnable contract. Sure, the club lead is a gamble, but the normal approach looks unlikely to succeed and when you have nothing to lose it is the perfect time to try something speculative.

active leads

It is time to look at the difference between 'Active' and 'Passive' leads. The club lead on the last hand was an Active lead. An alternative name would be an attacking lead. By their nature, such leads are dangerous. In other words, they risk giving declarer a trick that he could not make if left to his own devices.

Any lead of a small card from a suit headed by a broken honor holding is dangerous. Say that you lead low from KJ632. If partner holds either the ace or queen this will be a very effective lead. But you could just as easily be leading round into declarer's ace, queen. Now he will win a trick with the queen when, had you not led the suit he could never have done so, your king being poised over it and waiting to pounce. Nonetheless, attacking leads are sometimes necessary and, particularly in no trump contracts, even if they give away a trick at the start, if your suit is eventually established that trick may come back with interest. A case of speculating to accumulate.

The best time to make an attacking or Active lead is when you think that left to himself declarer will find enough tricks to bring home his contract so that at worst all you are doing is giving him an overtrick. The stronger the opposing auction the more likely that is to be the case. For example:

North	South
1♥	3♣
3♥	3NT
Pass	

Prospects for the defense are not good. Dummy has both an opening bid and a long suit which may provide several tricks. Meanwhile, declarer has shown not only a long suit of his own but also something around 16+ HCP – and the less high cards he holds the stronger will be his suit in compensation.

Such an auction cries out for an attacking lead as declarer will surely have more than enough tricks given the time to establish them. The opening leader should have no qualms at all about leading from a broken honor holding. Looking at:

♠ 864
♥ 97
♦ K10853
♣ Q72

a low diamond is the best hope for the defense. Maybe, if partner has a high diamond and a heart stopper so that declarer needs to bring in the club suit, you might have a chance this way. Make a passive lead such as a spade and declarer will have all the time in the world to find nine tricks.

On the same auction, what would you lead from:

♠ 9854
♥ Q54
♦ Q64
♣ 1083

Both enemy suits appear to be lying ominously well for declarer. Your ♥Q looks to be a dead duck while any club honor in partner's hand is also badly placed. This contract is likely to succeed whatever you lead but the best chance of beating it comes from the lead of a low diamond. With no long suit of your own you are trying to hit partner with a five card suit. He is a little more likely to hold five diamonds than five spades and, more to the point, you have more help in diamonds so have a better chance of establishing the suit quickly. The diamond lead is a piece of serious wishful thinking, but it really does look to be the only chance.

Even when the opposition have not bid particularly strongly, it can sometimes sound as though suits are breaking kindly for them and their finesses working. Take this auction:

North	South
1♥	2♣
2♥	2NT
3NT	Pass

North made a minimum rebid and South's 2NT was not a forcing bid so the contract has been reached with nothing to spare. Holding:

♠ 863
♥ AQ3
♦ K64
♣ 8432

however, prospects once again look bleak for the defense. As in the previous example, your heart honors look badly placed. Any club honors your side owns are also on the wrong side of the club bid, and if declarer needs a long suit to divide evenly it looks as though it will do so. Once again it is time to attack with a diamond lead and hope to hit partner's length.

passive leads

A Passive lead is a defensive or safe lead, one which may not achieve anything particularly dynamic from the defense's point of view but which is unlikely to give declarer anything he couldn't have done for himself.

A solid honor sequence is the perfect safe lead. If you lead king from KQJ, you either win or establish tricks for your side without giving declarer anything extra. Indeed, a solid sequence is ideal because it is both a safe lead and an attacking one.

An interior sequence is much less safe, requiring partner to hold an honor card if it is not to risk giving away a trick. The jack from KJ109 is a better lead than the two from KJ72, but it is still dangerous, needing the ace or queen from partner. Ten from Q1098 is a little better because now any one of three missing honors in partner's hand may prove sufficient.

The other really Passive lead is to lead from three or four small cards. The very worst this can do is to solve a two-way guess for declarer who might otherwise have finessed into partner's hand and lost a trick to, say, the queen. Otherwise, leading from a collection of small cards may not achieve very much but at least will probably do no harm.

When might you consider a Passive lead? The best time is when the opposition have struggled into their contract and sound to have nothing to spare. For example:

North	South
Pass	1NT
2NT	3NT
Pass	

Here, both declarer and dummy are known to hold fairly balanced hands and cannot have more than 25 or 26 HCP between them. With no long suit to work on declarer may not find it easy to come to nine tricks. The last thing you want to do is to give him a cheap trick on the opening lead. Look at these hands:

> ♠ KJ873
> ♥ Q54
> ♦ A97
> ♣ 73

Lead a low spade. True, this could give a trick, but it will work very well if partner has the ace or queen and even if he does not you may still be able to establish three tricks in spades as soon as one of you gets the lead.

> ♠ KJ42
> ♥ Q63
> ♦ A84
> ♣ 985

Now a club lead is more attractive, trying to give nothing away. The difference here is that, if you give a trick by leading a low spade, the best you can then hope to do is to establish two tricks later. So the return on your investment (the trick you gave declarer) is much less than in the previous example. Lead passively and make declarer do his own work.

♠ J109
♥ 73
♦ A8
♣ Q8643

Slightly more contentious than the previous example, perhaps, in that you do hold a five card suit plus an outside entry, making a low club quite plausible. Consider, however, that the opposition bid to 3NT without checking for a major-suit fit. Chances are that partner will be shortish in clubs as North, at least, is unlikely to hold a four-card major. So a club lead is quite likely to cost a trick in a dubious cause while the ♠J can never give a trick away and at worst will cost a tempo.

And here, although the opposition may have some spare values, the cards look to be lying very badly for them:

North	South
1 ♠	2 ♣
2 ♥	3NT
Pass	

You hold:

♠ 6
♥ 85
♦ K10762
♣ KJ975

Consider that declarer has heard North bid both majors yet has chosen to jump to 3NT. Surely South has a good diamond holding and thinks there can be no eight card major-suit fit.

South's actions plus your own hand make it clear that your partner is long in both majors. If he also has some high cards in the majors there may be no suit declarer can play on that will prove to be a rich source of tricks. After all, you seem to have both minors sewn up rather nicely, don't you?

All this points to leading as safely as possible. A diamond is very likely to be into declarer's ace, queen and a club is out for the same reason. It is highly unusual to lead a singleton against a no trump contract but this may be the time for it. If you lead your spade or, a good alternative, a heart, you hope that either partner or declarer will eventually lead the minor suits to you and you will make your honor cards. What you do not want to do is to give declarer a cheap trick when it looks as though he is going to have his work cut out if left to himself.

One more time when you might choose to lead from three or four small rather than a broken four card suit is if declarer opens 1NT and is left to play there. Against 1NT there is often time to change the direction of your attack later in the play if it seems that you picked the wrong suit with which to start off. That being the case, you might prefer to try to avoid giving a trick away at the start if you can find a

safe alternative. And remember, if you lead a high
spot card, e.g. seven from 8743, partner will know
that you are not really interested in the suit led so
will look to switch when he gains the lead.

While it is a close decision whether to lead a heart
or a spade against 1NT passed out from:

♠ 863
♥ K1086
♦ J53
♣ A92

it is clearly correct to lead a spade from:

♠ QJ10
♥ AJ53
♦ 964
♣ J82

The spade lead is so safe and, if it happens to hit
partner's length, will also prove to be a highly
effective attacking play.

lead-directing doubles

Before we leave leading against no trump
contracts there is one special way in which partner
can help us that must be mentioned.

Take these auctions:

(a)

West	North	East	South
Pass	1 ♦	Pass	2 ♣
2 ♥	3 ♦	Pass	3NT
Pass	Pass	Dble	All Pass

(b)

West	North	East	South
Pass	1 ♦	Pass	1 ♥
Pass	1 ♠	Pass	1NT
Pass	2NT	Pass	3NT
Pass	Pass	Dble	All Pass

There is nothing in either auction to suggest that partner can have so much strength that he knows he can defeat the contract. Conventionally, a double of a freely bid 3NT contract is lead-directing. In other words, partner thinks that, if you get off to the right opening lead, then he will have a good chance of beating the contract, while if you are left to yourself you are unlikely to find the lead he needs.

The normal agreement is that:

(i)   If either defender has bid a suit, that is the lead which the double requests.

(ii) If both defenders have bid but two different suits, the double asks the opening leader to lead his own suit. Normally, you would tend to lead partner's unless your suit was very good.

(iii) If neither defender has bid, the double asks for a lead of dummy's first bid suit –

unless the rest of the auction makes this clearly ridiculous, in which case you might try the second suit instead.

So the double in sequence (a) would ask for a heart lead, the suit you overcalled. Expect partner to hold a top heart honor plus at least one other good card somewhere.

The double in sequence (b) asks for a diamond, dummy's first bid suit but one which might still be only three or four cards in length. This would make an ideal doubling hand on auction (b):

♠ K103
♥ 84
♦ AQ1097
♣ 863

Note that not only does partner relish a diamond lead, he also has a real dislike for a club – the unbid suit and thus your most likely choice without the double.

Actually, with the opposition having only just staggered into game on minimum values, and with the cards seemingly very badly placed for declarer, 3NT doubled could easily go two or three down and give you a very healthy penalty.

leads against suit contracts

In a no trump contract, you were willing to give away a trick on the opening lead in the hope that it would come back later, with interest, if you could exhaust declarer of winners in your suit. This was quite a reasonable gamble because there was only one way in which declarer could stop you from cashing winners in your suit, namely by playing high cards in it. But in a suit contract there is a second way in which declarer can stem the flow of your winners; he can use a trump.

Because of this, it is rare for the defense to be able to establish a long suit and then cash several winners in it. This will only be possible when you have exhausted declarer not only of high cards in your suit but also of trumps. Accordingly, to give declarer a cheap trick at the start is often too high a price to pay as you will get little or no return on your investment. As a trick given away at this stage may never be recovered, your opening lead style should generally be more cautious, or passive, than against no trump.

As always, if partner has bid a suit that is a good indication that he may have strength in it and that will usually make it a good lead, both safe and attacking in that you can hope to cash or establish winners quickly.

Conversely, if it is your opponents who have bid a suit, you will rarely do well by leading it unless, perhaps, your lead is a short suit and you hope to get a chance to trump the next round.

Whether in an unbid suit or in a side-suit bid by the opposition, the weaker your all-round hand, the more attractive is the lead of a short suit. This is because if it is to prove effective your partner must be able to gain the lead to return the suit for you to ruff. Obviously, the weaker your hand the more strength is left for your partner to hold, and hence the more entries he is likely to have.

The other factor to consider when leading a short suit is your trump holding. There is no point in leading a singleton if you hold, say, ace, king doubleton trump. They are sure tricks already so trumping will gain absolutely nothing. A good trump holding to have when looking for a ruff is ace doubleton or ace to three cards. These are attractive holdings because even if partner cannot win the first trick and fire back a card for you to ruff, you will be in a position to win the first round of trumps and try to find an entry in partner's hand so that he can now give the desired ruff.

While it should not bar you from leading a singleton, a holding of only two or three small trumps is less likely to be effective. The reason is that, without trump control, there is a danger of declarer being able to win the opening lead and to draw all your trumps before you can get in.

Generally, however, a singleton is quite a good lead against a suit contract and, of course, it is a lead you would hardly ever even consider against no trump.

When leading an unbid suit, you should usually try to find a safe lead. Sequences of touching honor cards are, as always, ideal, because even when you do not win the first trick you give declarer nothing he could not do for himself and you also have the potential to establish winners for your own side.

Leading from holdings such as Axxx, Kxxx, Qxxx, and Jxxx are all dangerous as they risk allowing declarer to make a trick with a card which would not have been a winner had you not led the suit. The addition of a second honor such as KJxx or Q10xx improves things a little as you now need less help from partner for the lead to be effective but there is still a real danger of giving away a cheap trick for which you will never get any compensation. Any of these leads can be successful and will be correct on certain hands, but all are risky.

More dangerous still are leads of doubleton honors such as Kx or Qx in unbid suits. Such leads will be spectacularly successful on occasions but far more often will just throw away a trick. And the same applies to leading suits headed by the ace but not the king. Axx, Axxx and AJx are suits to be avoided if there is any plausible alternative. Again, there is too big a risk of giving declarer a cheap trick. If you do feel it appropriate to lead a suit such as Axxx, lead the ace rather than a small card. At least that way you will make a trick while a low card could whistle round to declarer's bare king, for example. But, as I say, try to avoid leading the suit at all. If you lead out an ace, most of the time you will just collect an assortment of small cards on it. Wait for someone else to lead the suit and you may capture a king or queen, a far more efficient use of your high card.

A very good lead is a top card from a suit headed by both the ace and king. You get to win the trick, see dummy and partner's signal, and still have the lead so can decide what to do next. A special conventional play is to lead the king from ace, king doubleton, a reversal of the normal play. When you then follow with the ace on the next round partner should realise that you had a reason for playing your cards in this unusual order. You have, as this play shows specifically ace, king doubleton and if partner gains the lead when you switch at trick three he will know that you can ruff the third round of the suit.

As in no trump, the bidding offers valuable pointers as to what kind of lead to make. We have already seen that a suit bid by partner is generally a good choice. But even when he has not bid there will be other clues. Take this hand:

♠ K2
♥ 874
♦ 875
♣ 109853

Suppose that I asked you, 'What would you lead from this hand against 4 ♥?' Whatever card you chose I would tell you that your answer was incorrect, unless you had first asked me about the bidding to get to 4 ♥. Take this auction:

South	North
1 ♥	1NT
3 ♥	4 ♥
Pass	

The opposition have reached game via an invitational sequence – North could have passed 3 ♥. They will not have many spare values and the auction offers no evidence that dummy will have a long or strong side-suit on which declarer might be able to discard his losers. It is not clear where four defensive tricks are going to come from but there is no reason to panic. Make a safe lead – the ♣10, top of a sequence, is the obvious choice – and leave declarer to do his own work.

Now look at this auction:

South	North
1♥	3♦
3NT	4♥
Pass	

Things are quite different this time. The opposition are known to have a good trump fit, and you can see that the trumps are breaking kindly for declarer. The strong jump shift of 3♦ tells you that dummy not only has a lot of high card strength but also a good long suit. Both red suits seem to be dividing evenly and it seems that declarer should have no trouble in coming to ten tricks if left to himself.

That being the case, you have little to lose by making an attacking lead. The best chance of defeating 4♥ is to lead the ♠K and hope to find partner with the ace. If you can take ♠K, ♠A and a spade ruff, partner will need only one more trick for you to beat the game. More often than not, partner will not have what you need. In that case your aggressive lead may give an overtrick or perhaps make no difference at all. But you make such a big profit by defeating the game that, even if your lead only succeeds one time in ten, it will still be handsomely rewarded in the long run.

This is the sort of lay-out you are hoping for:

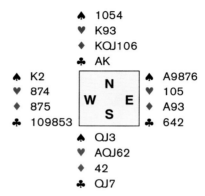

♠ 1054
♥ K93
♦ KQJ106
♣ AK

♠ K2
♥ 874
♦ 875
♣ 109853

♠ A9876
♥ 105
♦ A93
♣ 642

♠ QJ3
♥ AQJ62
♦ 42
♣ QJ7

If you don't get your ruff immediately, declarer will be able to draw trumps and you will have only the three top tricks to take.

There is one other type of lead which, for fairly obvious reasons, is unique to suit contracts. It is to lead a trump. The time to consider a trump lead is when dummy has supported declarer's suit, showing that he genuinely likes it. If dummy has a shortage in another suit, there is a danger that declarer will be able to make extra tricks by ruffing in the dummy. In such cases, a trump lead may prove to be effective, cutting down the number of trumps in dummy and so the number of times that dummy can ruff.

Beginners, as I have already mentioned, tend to be too eager to take their own winners quickly and so overlook the possibility of leading trumps as they see little prospect of winning tricks by doing so. But, taking a longer-term view, preventing declarer from making tricks is just as effective as winning tricks yourself. Eventually it comes to the same thing. Better to take four tricks late in the play than only three at the beginning.

A trump lead temporarily gives up the initiative, handing over the lead and control of the play to declarer. If dummy has a good side-suit, declarer may be able to pitch his losers before you regain the lead. For this reason it is important to listen to the bidding and not overdo the trump leads. Trump leads are attractive when:

(i)   The bidding suggests that dummy has both trump support and a shapely hand.
(ii) When the defenders have the bulk of the high cards. Now declarer will need to do a lot of ruffing to make tricks.
(iii) When every other lead looks too dangerous.

Conversely, a trump lead is unattractive if:

(i)   Dummy has not shown any support.
(ii) Dummy has shown a good side-suit on which declarer might be able to take discards.

(iii) When you have four or more reasonable trumps. You may do better to lead something else and try to make declarer ruff, eventually hoping to have more trumps than he has.

(iv) When you have a singleton trump and no reason to imagine that the opposition have a very big fit. Now it is possible that partner has four trumps and again the defense of trying to force declarer to ruff may prove effective. Even if declarer cannot be forced, a trump lead may mess up partner's trump holding, making it easier for declarer to pick it up for minimum loss.

But even these points should only be considered to be guidelines rather than absolute rules. You still need to use some judgement. Take this auction:

South	West	North	East
3♣	Dble	5♣	Dble
All Pass			

Both you and partner have shown good hands. The only way declarer is likely to get close to his contract is by cross-ruffing. Even a singleton trump is a good lead. You want to cut down the ruffs as much as possible.

And on auctions where the opposition are clearly sacrificing at a high level, a trump is usually correct.

South	West	North	East
Pass	1♠	2♣	3♦
5♣	5♦	6♣	Dble
All Pass			

Holding:

♠ KQJ94
♥ AQJ
♦ Q87
♣ 74

Don't even think about leading your spade sequence. There is no hurry. You have spades, partner has diamonds, and you have the hearts sewn up. Declarer has only one source of tricks – clubs – and the sooner you can draw trumps the better. Clearly the opposition must have some distribution to bid so high on a low point-count, but an opening trump lead and a second round when you regain the lead should leave them struggling.

At lower levels a trump may be correct simply because it seems safest. Consider these two auctions:

(a)

South	North
1♥	1NT
2♥	Pass

(b)   *South   North*
               1 ♥   2 ♥
               Pass

On the first auction, declarer is known to have a long suit but there is no reason to think that dummy has any trump support or will be able to ruff anything. It could still be right to lead a trump but only for want of anything safer.

♠ KJ3
♥ 1098
♦ AJ64
♣ K103

Why try to guess in which side-suit partner has strength? A wrong guess could give away a trick which will never return. The ♥10 is hardly dynamic but at worst it saves declarer from using up a dummy entry to take a heart finesse. With your all-round strength, you will have plenty of opportunity to make more attacking plays later in the hand.

On the second auction, the opposition are known to have a fit. Not only is no other suit attractive, all being very dangerous, but now you have a positive reason to lead a trump as well as a negative one, you would like to cut down on dummy's ruffing potential.

Change your hand a little to:

♠ KJ3
♥ 94
♦ AJ64
♣ K1052

Your heart holding is no longer a sequence and hence it does not offer quite such a safe lead. I would still recommend a trump on the second auction, where dummy is known to have trump support, even though this may solve a guess for declarer.

On the first auction, where dummy may be very short in hearts and partner have a useful four card holding, there is a serious danger of a trump lead chewing up his holding to declarer's advantage. Though nothing else is attractive either, partner will never forgive you if you pick up his trumps for declarer and I would be inclined to try a low club instead. Of course, that could prove wrong if partner has no club honor but you have to lead something.

leading against slams

Leading against a slam, whether in no trumps or a suit, is quite a different matter to leading against a game or part-score.

Firstly, consider the situation when your opponents bid a grand slam. They are trying to make all thirteen tricks so, unless they have had a disaster in the bidding, they will surely hold all the aces. Unless partner is able to ruff the opening lead, you will not be able to win the opening trick. What you should try to do is to lead as safely as possible. It would be crazy to lead away from a high honor to try to establish tricks for your side. If you get in to cash them you will have beaten the hand anyway. Your only hope is to try to give nothing away and pray that declarer must finesse into your high card.

The opposition bid: 2NT – 7NT and you must lead from:

$$\spadesuit \quad 1098$$
$$\heartsuit \quad K754$$
$$\diamondsuit \quad 8654$$
$$\clubsuit \quad 75$$

Lead the ♠10, your sequence, and just hope that declarer has the ♥A and doesn't have thirteen tricks without taking the finesse. A heart lead could give him a cheap trick and that could be the thirteenth.

You may be able to make an attacking lead but only in an attempt to give partner a ruff.

South	North
1♠	3NT
4♦	4♥(i)
4NT(ii)	5♥(iii)
7♦	7♠
Pass	

(i)   Ace of hearts
(ii) Blackwood
(iii) Two aces

You hold:

♠ 86
♥ J1098
♦ 87643
♣ K5

You have a perfectly safe heart lead, courtesy of your sequence, but declarer has shown a big two-suited hand with spades and diamonds and dummy responded 3NT so should be balanced. It is no certainty, but there is a distinct possibility that partner will be void in diamonds. As it can hardly cost a trick and nothing else looks likely to succeed, try a diamond. You never know, you might get lucky.

And the same general rule applies when your opponents bid to 6NT. Unless they have shown long suits which appear to be breaking kindly, when a passive defense may be inadequate, you should usually look to lead as passively as possible. After the auction:

South	North
2NT	4NT
6NT	Pass

Your lead from:

♠ KJ764
♥ J109
♦ 764
♣ Q3

should be ♥J, the safest lead you can find. Against 3NT you would have led a low spade, hoping to find partner with help in the suit to enable you to establish several winners for when you regained the lead. But in 6NT you don't need several tricks, you need two. And if your opponents, both of whom sound to hold balanced hands, have bid up to 6NT when you hold 7 HCP, how likely is it that partner has any high cards? Best to lead a heart and pray that declarer takes two black finesses into your hand.

If competent opponents bid six of a suit contract, the assumption is that they know what they are doing and will normally have twelve tricks if they don't lose two first. Take this auction:

South	North
1♠	3♦
3♠	4NT(i)
5♥ (ii)	6♠
Pass	

(i) Blackwood
(ii) Two aces

Suppose that you have to lead from:

♠ 76
♥ K876
♦ 653
♣ 10987

The auction sounds strong and confident, with dummy having a long strong side-suit plus support for declarer's spades. If you cannot cash or establish two tricks very quickly it sounds as though the slam will come home.

The best lead is a low heart. It is not so much that you expect to find partner with the ace, though North may be gambling that you will not find the lead, but more likely is that partner may have ♥Q and if declarer has to take a diamond finesse to partner's king, or partner has the ♠A, you hope to establish the second trick before declarer can set up his own winners.

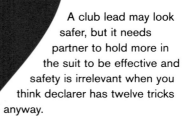

A club lead may look safer, but it needs partner to hold more in the suit to be effective and safety is irrelevant when you think declarer has twelve tricks anyway.

A singleton may also be a good lead, though it risks trapping partner's honors in the suit. It will be extremely effective, however, if partner has either the ace of the suit led or the ace of trumps with which to gain the lead. You may be able to judge how likely that is from the auction. To lead a singleton in declarer or dummy's main side-suit can be very dangerous as it helps to establish the suit, doing declarer's work for him.

the lightner double

What is going on on this deal?

West	North	East	South
Pass	1 ♥	Pass	2 ♠
Pass	3 ♠	Pass	4NT(i)
Pass	5 ♦ (ii)	Pass	6 ♠
Pass	Pass	Dble	All Pass

(i)   Blackwood
(ii) One ace

You are looking at:

♠ 7
♥ 108763
♦ QJ109
♣ K53

What would you lead?

Left to yourself you would no doubt have chosen
♦Q as being both safe and having potential to
establish winners if partner has the ace or king.
But what is partner's double about?

He can hardly be looking at two aces, for example,
so cannot be doubling on two sure tricks. The
conventional meaning of a double of a freely bid
slam is that it is lead-directing. In other words,
partner has a special feature in his hand
which makes him think that if you find the
right lead he might be able to beat the
contract. What can that special
feature be? Given your heart
length, a heart void is likely. So
lead a low heart expecting
partner to ruff and, hopefully,
cash an ace for one down.

The name given to this type of
lead-directing double is a Lightner Double,
after the American expert, Theodore
Lightner, who first suggested the idea.

summing up

So to sum up. As a general principle you should attack against a small slam in a suit, lead passively against a grand slam or 6NT. Against lower level suit contracts, tend to be fairly cautious unless the auction suggests that declarer will have plenty of tricks if given time to enjoy them. Against no trump, be more inclined to attack, certainly if you have a long suit to lead plus entry cards.

But, whatever the contract, listen to how it was reached. There is a wealth of clues in the auction if you know what to look out for. The stronger the auction, the more reason to attack, the weaker, the more reason to go passive.

The remainder of this book consists of a series of exercises. See if you can find the recommended leads, and for the right reasons, then work through the answers. Take confidence from those examples where you agree with the recommended answer. Where you disagree, think it through again and see if you can understand the point behind the hand.

The opening lead, as I said at the beginning, is one of the most difficult areas of the game. But if you gather together all the clues from the auction and think it through clearly, you should be able to make yourself a good and effective player in this important aspect of the game.

quiz one

In each case, which card would you lead from this suit?

1. *Against a No Trump Contract*

    (i)   A108632
    (ii)   875
    (iii)   K1098
    (iv)   QJ108
    (v)   Q643
    (vi)   AKJ109

2. *Against a Suit Contract*

    (vii)   74
    (viii) QJ97
    (ix)   A863
    (x)   AK
    (xi)   AK74
    (xii)   KJ762

solutions

In each case, what would you lead from this suit?

1. Against a No Trump Contract

    (i)   **A108632**

The six is correct, fourth highest from a suit headed by an honor.

    (ii)   **875**

The seven, second highest from three or more small cards with no honor.

    (iii)   **K1098**

Lead the ten, the top card of the interior sequence.

    (iv)   **QJ108**

The queen, top of the sequence.

    (v)   **Q643**

The three, fourth highest from a suit headed by an honor.

    (vi)   **AKJ109**

Lead the ace, asking partner to throw the queen if he has it or, failing that, signal whether he has an odd or even number of cards in the suit.

2. *Against a Suit Contract*

(vii)   **74**

Lead the seven, top of a doubleton. It is only from three or more low cards that you lead the second highest.

(viii)   **QJ97**

Though not quite solid, the QJ9 qualifies as a sequence, so lead the queen, the top card.

(ix)   **A863**

Lead the ace. An unsupported ace is rarely an attractive lead against a suit contract but once you have decided that this is the suit to lead then the ace is the correct card. Note that against no trump you would prefer to lead your fourth best card.

(x)   **AK**

Lead the king followed by the ace. This reversal of the normal order is a special play which informs partner that you hold precisely ace, king doubleton.

(xi)   **AK74**

This time you should lead the ace. Ace from a suit headed by ace and king is a good lead because you retain the lead and can choose to continue the suit or switch, depending on what you see at trick one.

(xii)   **KJ762**

Lead the six. Just as in no trump, the fourth highest card is correct from a suit headed by a broken honor holding.

quiz two

You are West. In each case, what would you lead on the auction given?

1.
- ♠ 94
- ♥ Q7652
- ♦ A73
- ♣ J42

(a)

West	North	East	South
Pass	1♦	Pass	1NT
All Pass			

(b)

West	North	East	South
Pass	1♦	1♠	1NT
All Pass			

2.
- ♠ A7
- ♥ 8
- ♦ Q9742
- ♣ 108432

(a)

West	North	East	South
Pass	1♣	Pass	1♠
Pass	2♠	Pass	4♠
All Pass			

(b)

West	North	East	South
Pass	1♦	Pass	1♠
Pass	2♥	Pass	3♦
Pass	3♠	Pass	4♠
All Pass			

3.

- ♠ A543
- ♥ 4
- ♦ Q1098
- ♣ K632

(a)

West	North	East	South
Pass	1♣	Pass	1♥
Pass	2♥	Pass	4♥
All Pass			

(b)

West	North	East	South
Pass	1♦	Pass	1♥
Pass	3♥	Pass	4♥
All Pass			

4.

- ♠ J874
- ♥ 1098
- ♦ 763
- ♣ KQ8

(a)

West	North	East	South
Pass	Pass	Pass	1NT
Pass	2NT	Pass	3NT
All Pass			

(b)	West	North	East	South
	–	–	Pass	1NT
	Pass	3♦	Pass	3♥
	Pass	3NT	All Pass	

5.

    ♠ 743
    ♥ A63
    ♦ Q84
    ♣ KJ63

(a)	West	North	East	South
	Pass	Pass	Pass	1♠
	Pass	2♠	Pass	4♠
	All Pass			

(b)	West	North	East	South
	–	–	Pass	1♠
	Pass	3♦	Pass	3♠
	Pass	4♠	All Pass	

6.

    ♠ J3
    ♥ QJ642
    ♦ 1098
    ♣ A54

(a)	West	North	East	South
	Pass	Pass	Pass	1NT
	Pass	2♣	Pass	2♦
	Pass	3NT	All Pass	

(b)

West	North	East	South
Pass	1♥	Pass	2NT
Pass	3NT	All Pass	

7.

♠ J643
♥ K832
♦ 1097
♣ 65

(a)

West	North	East	South
–	–	Pass	2NT
Pass	6NT	All Pass	

(b)

West	North	East	South
–	–	Pass	1♦
Pass	3♣	Pass	3♦
Pass	4NT(i)	Pass	5♥(ii)
Pass	6♦	All Pass	

(i) Blackwood
(ii) Two aces

8.

♠ KJ762
♥ 73
♦ QJ10
♣ K42

(a)

West	North	East	South
Pass	Pass	Pass	1NT
Pass	3NT	All Pass	

	West	North	East	South
	Pass	Pass	Pass	1NT
	Pass	2♣	Pass	2♥
	Pass	2NT	Pass	3NT
	All Pass			

9.

♠ 74
♥ Q63
♦ 9862
♣ KJ64

(a)	West	North	East	South
	Pass	1♥	Pass	1♠
	Pass	2♥	Pass	3♠
	Pass	4♠	All Pass	

(b)	West	North	East	South
	Pass	Pass	Pass	1♥
	Pass	1♠	Pass	2♣
	Pass	2♥	Pass	3♥
	Pass	4♥	All Pass	

10.

♠ 764
♥ 5
♦ AQ1072
♣ AQJ5

(a)	West	North	East	South
	–	–	–	1NT
	Pass	2♣	Pass	2♠
	Pass	3♠	Pass	4♠
	All Pass			

(b)	West	North	East	South
	–	1♦	Pass	1♠
	Pass	2♠	Pass	3NT
	Pass	4♠	All Pass	

solutions

You are West. In each case, what would you lead on the auction given?

1.
♠ 94
♥ Q7652
♦ A73
♣ J42

(a)	West	North	East	South
	Pass	1♦	Pass	1NT
	All Pass			

There is no reason to look further than your five card heart suit, hoping that partner can help to establish long tricks there. Conventionally, you would lead the fourth highest card, the ♥5.

(b)	West	North	East	South
	Pass	1♦	1♠	1NT
	All Pass			

Partner's 1♠ overcall makes quite a big difference to your choice of opening lead. You are trying to lead the suit in which your side has the best combined holding and therefore the best chance of establishing several tricks. As the overcall promises a reasonable five card or longer suit, spades is the suit you should lead, choosing the ♠9, top of a doubleton.

2.

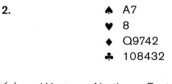

♠ A7
♥ 8
♦ Q9742
♣ 108432

(a)	West	North	East	South
	Pass	1♣	Pass	1♠
	Pass	2♠	Pass	4♠
	All Pass			

This is the ideal time to lead your singleton, hoping to get a ruff. You have trump control so that even if partner does not hold the ♥A you will be able to win the first round of trumps and try to give him the lead in whichever minor suit seems appropriate. Note that the weaker your all-round hand, the more likely partner is to have some high cards and therefore an entry.

(b)

West	North	East	South
Pass	1 ♦	Pass	1 ♠
Pass	2 ♥	Pass	3 ♦
Pass	3 ♠	Pass	4 ♠
All Pass			

The singleton heart lead could still prove to be effective but this time there is a much more promising option. North has reversed, showing five diamonds. In fact his sequence strongly suggests 3-4-5-1 distribution. South has shown diamond preference by bidding 3 ♦, and you are looking at five cards in diamonds. It would not be all that surprising if partner were to be void in diamonds, and he can hardly have more than a singleton.

Rather than lead a heart in the hope of getting a ruff yourself, why not lead a diamond with the certainty of giving partner at least one ruff? You will still be able to get a heart ruff yourself if partner either holds the ♥A or ruffs a diamond and returns a heart. When you win ♠A and give him a second diamond ruff he can then give you your ruff.

3.
- ♠ A543
- ♥ 4
- ♦ Q1098
- ♣ K632

(a)

West	North	East	South
Pass	1♣	Pass	1♥
Pass	2♥	Pass	4♥
All Pass			

A singleton trump is not an attractive lead as it risks catching partner's holding for declarer. Neither is a club that attractive as dummy has bid the suit, albeit in an auction which is quite consistent with 1♣ being a three or four card suit in a balanced hand, a better minor bid.

The real choice is between the two unbid suits and a diamond is much the better option. Spades are unattractive because the lead of a suit headed by an unsupported ace gives away a trick far too often. Meanwhile, any diamond honour in partner's hand could make a diamond lead successful, establishing winners for when the defense regains the lead. The correct card is the ♦10, top of the interior sequence.

(b)

West	North	East	South
Pass	1♦	Pass	1♥
Pass	3♥	Pass	4♥
All Pass			

A trump lead is still unattractive but this time
dummy has bid diamonds, suggesting that there
will not be many defensive tricks coming in that
suit. The choice comes down to the two black suits
and, while quite dangerous, a club lead is better
than a spade, being effective when partner holds
either the ace or queen, whereas a spade lead
needs to find partner with specifically the king. The
correct club to lead is the ♣2, fourth highest.

4.

♠	J874
♥	1098
♦	763
♣	KQ8

(a)

West	North	East	South
Pass	Pass	Pass	1NT
Pass	2NT	Pass	3NT
All Pass			

The opposition have both shown balanced hands
and have staggered into game, clearly with nothing
to spare. This is the classic time to defend
passively, trying to give nothing away and leave
declarer to do all his own work. A spade from that
scrappy suit could give a trick; better is the ♥10,
top of a sequence.

(b)

West	North	East	South
–	–	Pass	1NT
Pass	3♦	Pass	3♥
Pass	3NT	All Pass	

The same contract but a totally different auction. North's 3 ♦ is a strong bid and it promises a long suit. The opposition have plenty of high cards, a long suit which seems to be dividing well for them and your ♦ Q rates to be a dead duck. This is the time to attack.

Partner would need a lot of both length and strength for a heart or spade lead to be successful. The best chance of breaking this contract is to lead ♣K. It is still a long shot but what you hope is to find partner with either ♣Axxxx or ♣Jxxxx and a quick entry if declarer cannot run nine top tricks.

5.
- ♠ 743
- ♥ A63
- ♦ Q84
- ♣ KJ63

(a)	West	North	East	South
	Pass	Pass	Pass	1 ♠
	Pass	2 ♠	Pass	4 ♠
	All Pass			

The opposition have bid game easily enough but may not have much to spare given dummy's simple raise. Any sidesuit lead could be successful if you hit partner's strength but it could also be disastrous if it gives declarer a cheap trick.

There is nothing in the auction to suggest that dummy has a good suit on which declarer can throw his losers so there may be no need to make a dangerous attacking lead. Rather than guess which suit to try, lead a passive trump. Perhaps declarer needs to take several ruffs to fulfil his contract. You will surely gain the lead at some point and by then you hope to have more information to enable you to find the most effective continuation.

(b)

West	North	East	South
–	–	Pass	1♠
Pass	3♦	Pass	3♠
Pass	4♠	All Pass	

But this auction is very strong, with dummy having shown a big hand and a long strong side-suit before admitting to spade support. 4♠ will surely succeed unless the defense can get their tricks very quickly so the aggressive lead of a low club, the ♣3, is indicated, that being the suit in which you need the least help from partner.

6.

- ♠ J3
- ♥ QJ642
- ♦ 1098
- ♣ A54

(a)

West	North	East	South
Pass	Pass	Pass	1NT
Pass	2♣	Pass	2♦
Pass	3NT	All Pass	

Though both opponents are limited by their initial actions (or inaction in North's case), the auction has been a confident one. North used Stayman to ask opener for a four card major but the 2♦ response denied one.

North may hold four hearts but it is more likely that he was looking for a 4-4 spade fit. With the game having been bid confidently, an attacking lead seems indicated and the obvious choice is the five card heart suit, the ♥4 being the correct card, fourth best. While this will work out poorly if dummy does hold four hearts, no other lead is as likely to establish five defensive tricks in time to break the contract.

(b)	West	North	East	South
	Pass	1♥	Pass	2NT
	Pass	3NT	All Pass	

This time a heart would be a silly lead. Dummy has shown five cards in hearts and declarer a balanced hand. Partner is marked with a singleton heart or, just possibly, a void. In neither case will it be possible for you to get the hearts going. With nothing else looking particularly dynamic, a safe lead from the diamond sequence is best, so lead the ♦10.

7.

♠ J643
♥ K832
♦ 1097
♣ 65

(a)

West	North	East	South
–	–	Pass	2NT
Pass	6NT	All Pass	

When two balanced hands bid to 6NT they can only hope to make twelve tricks by sheer weight of high cards. This is not the time to make an aggressive lead in the hope of establishing tricks to cash later. Quite possibly declarer will have to play on all four suits before he has twelve tricks and your hope must be that this involves him in taking two losing finesses or something similar.

You want to find the safest lead possible and that is the ♦ 10, not a completely solid sequence but the next best thing.

(b)

West	North	East	South
–	–	Pass	1♦
Pass	3♣	Pass	3♦
Pass	4NT(i)	Pass	5♥(ii)
Pass	6♦	All Pass	
(i)	Blackwood		
(ii)	Two aces		

A very different auction with both opponents showing long suits which should produce plenty of tricks. This is the time to attack, as against most six level contracts in a suit, in the hope that you can cash or establish two defensive tricks before declarer can establish twelve. The suit in which you need least help from partner is hearts so that is the one you should lead, choosing the ♥2, fourth highest.

8.

      ♠ KJ762
      ♥ 73
      ♦ QJ10
      ♣ K42

(a)	West	North	East	South
	Pass	Pass	Pass	1NT
	Pass	3NT	All Pass	

A confident auction in which dummy has expressed no interest in finding a major suit fit. While a diamond lead might be safe, it rates to give a valuable tempo away, dummy having suggested some length in the minors by his failure to use Stayman. Best is to lead fourth highest of your long suit, the ♠6, and hope to find partner with a fitting honour to establish your suit.

(b)	West	North	East	South
	Pass	Pass	Pass	1NT
	Pass	2♣	Pass	2♥
	Pass	2NT	Pass	3NT
	All Pass			

The same contract but the Stayman auction has
been very revealing. Declarer has shown four
hearts but that did not interest dummy. It follows
that dummy must hold four spades, else why
bother to use the Stayman 2♣ bid?

Dummy also only made an invitational bid so
declarer will have nothing to spare. The auction
having made a spade lead unattractive, go for the
safe top of a sequence lead of the ♦Q.

9.

♠ 74
♥ Q63
♦ 9862
♣ KJ64

(a)	West	North	East	South
	Pass	1♥	Pass	1♠
	Pass	2♥	Pass	3♠
	Pass	4♠	All Pass	

Though declarer's 3♠ bid is only invitational, it seems
that both majors lie very favorably for him, with your
♥Q finessable and any spade honour in partner's
hand also badly placed from your point of view.

When things appear to be lying well for declarer
the assumption is that, left to himself, he should be
able to find the tricks he needs. Accordingly, the
defense must attack to try to get four tricks before
he can take ten. The best attacking lead is ♣4,
hoping to find partner with the ace or queen.

(b)	West	North	East	South
	Pass	Pass	Pass	1♥
	Pass	1♠	Pass	2♣
	Pass	2♥	Pass	3♥
	Pass	4♥	All Pass	

This time declarer's finesses all look as though
they may fail. He has bid hearts and clubs and all
your strength is in those suits, sitting over his
strength. Meanwhile dummy has bid spades, a suit
in which you hold nothing. Any spade finesses also
rate to fail.

Game was only reached after an invitational
sequence and with things lying badly it will prove an
uphill struggle for declarer. This is not the time to
attack, particularly as declarer has bid clubs, the
one suit in which you could make an attacking lead.
No, best to make a passive diamond lead and leave
declarer to get on with it. You would lead the ♦ 8,
second highest from an assortment of small cards.

10.　　　　　　　♠ 764
　　　　　　　　　♥ 5
　　　　　　　　　♦ AQ1072
　　　　　　　　　♣ AQJ5

(a)	West	North	East	South
	–	–	–	1NT
	Pass	2♣	Pass	2♠
	Pass	3♠	Pass	4♠
	All Pass			

Your first thought might be to lead the singleton heart, but is that actually likely to work? The opposition have bid happily up to game while you are sitting there with 13 HCP. Is it likely that partner has an entry with which to give you a heart ruff?

The answer, of course, is no. All a heart lead is likely to achieve is to pick up partner's ♥Qxxxx, ♥Q10xxx or ♥Jxxxx for declarer, perhaps giving him a crucial discard in another suit.

Neither minor suit offers an attractive lead, particularly as the stronger of the opposing hands is on your right. Best is a passive trump lead. If you continue to lead trumps each time you gain the lead declarer may find that he cannot take as many ruffs as he would like. Meanwhile, if he holds the minor suit kings and has to lead the suits himself, you will be well placed to pick them off with your aces and still retain the master cards in each suit, the two queens.

Which trump you lead is not all that important but the ♠6, intending to follow with the ♠4 on the next round, is technically correct. Signals in the trump suit are usually played in the reverse manner to any other suit so the high-low play suggests an odd number of trumps.

(b)	West	North	East	South
	–	1♦	Pass	1♠
	Pass	2♠	Pass	3NT
	Pass	4♠	All Pass	

The singleton lead is still unattractive for the same reasons as on the previous auction. A trump may again cause declarer some problems but the diamond bid suggests that this suit at least is lying well for him.

North has bid diamonds and declarer has shown a balanced hand with his leap to 3NT. Does that suggest anything? Precisely. Both opponents have some diamonds, a suit in which you also hold five. Partner may well be very short of diamonds and there is a good chance of giving him a ruff. Lead ace and a low diamond and if he can ruff and return a club that may be all that is required to beat the contract.

Even if partner is not ruffing the second diamond, the suit being distributed something like:

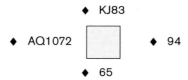

♦ KJ83

♦ AQ1072   ♦ 94

♦ 65

declarer is unlikely to have the nerve to finesse the jack on the second round, establishing a winner for a discard in another suit. Surely he will rise with the king, whereas, had you led a trump, his first diamond play might well have been low to the jack. When that holds it is not difficult to return to hand and lead a second round towards the king.

quiz three

On each of these hands, what would be your opening lead as West?

1.
West	North	East	South
Pass	Pass	Pass	1NT
All Pass			

(a)
- ♠ 987
- ♥ Q743
- ♦ A843
- ♣ 104

(b)
- ♠ J65
- ♥ 72
- ♦ A843
- ♣ K743

(c)
- ♠ QJ104
- ♥ K10853
- ♦ 98
- ♣ A4

2.
West	North	East	South
Pass	Pass	Pass	1♥
Pass	1♠	Pass	2♣
Pass	3♣	Pass	3♥
Pass	3♠	Pass	5♣
All Pass			

(a)
- ♠ 10987
- ♥ K5
- ♦ AQ64
- ♣ 863

(b)
- ♠ 72
- ♥ AQ104
- ♦ Q853
- ♣ A53

(c)
- ♠ 6
- ♥ 7653
- ♦ KQ1042
- ♣ K63

3.

West	North	East	South
Pass	1♦	Pass	1♠
Pass	2♠	Pass	4♠
All Pass			

(a)
- ♠ 764
- ♥ AK
- ♦ 10875
- ♣ J1098

(b)
- ♠ 1053
- ♥ AKJ
- ♦ 986
- ♣ Q532

(c)
- ♠ 74
- ♥ A1042
- ♦ 86
- ♣ Q7643

4.

West	North	East	South
–	–	1♥	1♠
3♥	4♠	All Pass	

(a)
- ♠ 53
- ♥ AQ74
- ♦ J108
- ♣ K842

(b)
- ♠ K54
- ♥ A1074
- ♦ 6
- ♣ J10987

(c)
- ♠ Q82
- ♥ Q97
- ♦ AJ875
- ♣ J7

5.

West	North	East	South
–	–	Pass	1♠
Pass	2♦	Pass	2♥
Pass	2NT	Pass	3♥
Pass	4♥	All Pass	

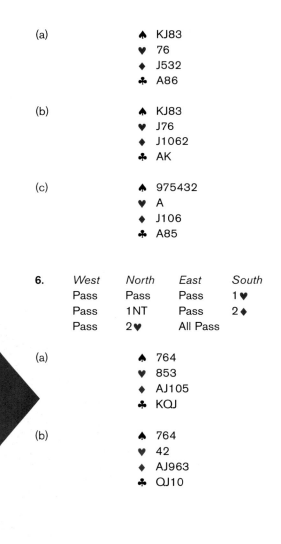

(a)
- ♠ KJ83
- ♥ 76
- ♦ J532
- ♣ A86

(b)
- ♠ KJ83
- ♥ J76
- ♦ J1062
- ♣ AK

(c)
- ♠ 975432
- ♥ A
- ♦ J106
- ♣ A85

6.

West	North	East	South
Pass	Pass	Pass	1♥
Pass	1NT	Pass	2♦
Pass	2♥	All Pass	

(a)
- ♠ 764
- ♥ 853
- ♦ AJ105
- ♣ KQJ

(b)
- ♠ 764
- ♥ 42
- ♦ AJ963
- ♣ QJ10

(c)
- ♠ 875
- ♥ Q4
- ♦ AJ104
- ♣ QJ97

solutions

On each of these hands, what would be your opening lead as West?

1.

West	North	East	South
Pass	Pass	Pass	1NT
All Pass			

(a)
- ♠ 987
- ♥ Q743
- ♦ A843
- ♣ 104

Had you a five card suit, you would normally lead it, but with a choice of scrappy four card suits, leading either of which could give a cheap trick, a passive spade lead looks better, the ♠8, second from three small. Against 1NT there should be plenty of time to switch to either red suit if necessary.

(b)
- ♠ J65
- ♥ 72
- ♦ A843
- ♣ K743

The hand looks similar to the previous one but there is a difference. The shorter the suit you are considering as an opening lead, the greater is the danger that you are going to hit one of declarer's suits and do some of his work for him.

Accordingly, a low doubleton is significantly less attractive than three or four small when looking to lead passively. Though the ♥7 could be the winner, you should choose between your four-card suits (♠J65 is a dangerous lead without the long-term benefit of establishing long cards) and, once you have made that decision, it is better to lead the stronger one, hence the ♦3.

(c)
- ♠ QJ104
- ♥ K10853
- ♦ 98
- ♣ A4

This time you do hold a five card suit but it is headed by a broken honor holding, so is a dangerous lead. Nonetheless, you would lead a heart were it not for the excellent alternative you have. The ♠Q is both safe and, because it is from a four card suit, will eventually establish your tricks rather than declarer's.

2.

West	North	East	South
Pass	Pass	Pass	1 ♥
Pass	1 ♠	Pass	2 ♣
Pass	3 ♣	Pass	3 ♥
Pass	3 ♠	Pass	5 ♣
All Pass			

(a)
- ♠ 10987
- ♥ K5
- ♦ AQ64
- ♣ 863

A spade lead looks safe and so, probably, will be a trump, but there is something better. The auction has been very revealing. Both opponents have clubs and each was prepared to repeat there major, yet no one was willing to bid no trump. Why? Because they have nothing in diamonds. Though it goes against the usual rules, this is a good time to lead a suit headed by the ace but not the king. Try the ace of diamonds, intending to follow up with a low one to partner's assumed king.

The trouble with a passive lead is that declarer may have two diamonds and a singleton spade. If you don't cash your diamonds immediately, he may be able to take discards on dummy's spades.

(b)
- ♠ 72
- ♥ AQ104
- ♦ Q853
- ♣ A53

The same reasoning might persuade you to lead a diamond from this hand also. However, it is not guaranteed that declarer cannot have ♦A or a shortage and there is something much more urgent for you to do. Looking at your hearts, you are very keen to prevent dummy from ruffing too often. Lead ace and another club, with the intention of leading a third round when you win the first round of hearts. With a bit of luck you will restrict declarer to just one heart ruff in the dummy and will have a second heart trick to come.

(c)
           ♠ 6
           ♥ 7653
           ♦ KQ1042
           ♣ K63

With weak hearts, there is no reason to lead a trump this time so it appears that you are back to leading a diamond. However, your spade singleton suggests that declarer will not be able to take quick discards and also that you may be able to take a spade ruff. Lead the singleton and hope to win the ♣K then put partner in with a diamond to give you your ruff.

An initial diamond lead may mean that you no longer have the communications to get your ruff.

3.	West	North	East	South
	Pass	1♦	Pass	1♠
	Pass	2♠	Pass	4♠
	All Pass			

(a)
- ♠ 764
- ♥ AK
- ♦ 10875
- ♣ J1098

A club lead will be safe and is quite attractive but it may take too long to develop club tricks. Best is to cash both hearts then try to give partner the lead. Perhaps he will then be able to give you a heart ruff. To let him know that you have precisely ace, king doubleton, lead the king, intending to follow with the ace unless the sight of dummy suggests that you need to think again.

(b)
- ♠ 1053
- ♥ AKJ
- ♦ 986
- ♣ Q532

Again hearts offers the best prospects for the defense. This time, however, you should lead the normal ace. After seeing dummy and partner's signal, you may choose to continue hearts or to switch to another suit and wait for partner to get in to lead a second heart through declarer's hypothetical queen to allow you to trap it.

(c)
- ♠ 74
- ♥ A1042
- ♦ 86
- ♣ Q7643

An unsupported ace is not such a good lead so hearts are out this time. A low club is possible but your lack of intermediates to back up the queen suggests that, even if partner has the king, you may not only establish a trick for your side but also for declarer. This is the layout that you are worried about:

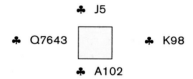

♣ J5

♣ Q7643   ♣ K98

♣ A102

Left to himself, declarer will make only one club trick. If you lead low to the king and ace, however, he can return the suit to establish his ten for a discard in dummy.

There is also the possibility that declarer may hold something like ♣KJ5 opposite two low in the dummy. If you lead the suit partner will win his ace but then declarer has the king; if you wait for someone else to lead clubs declarer has to guess who has the ace and who the queen and will lose two tricks if he guesses wrong.

A doubleton in dummy's first bid suit is also uninspiring and overall a passive low trump lead looks best, leaving declarer to do all his own work in the side-suits.

4.	West	North	East	South
	–	–	1 ♥	1 ♠
	3 ♥	4 ♠	All Pass	

(a)
- ♠ 53
- ♥ AQ74
- ♦ J108
- ♣ K842

Lead the ace of hearts. There is no other lead which stands out and it would be very unlucky to find that this gave away the vital trick, given that partner opened 1 ♥, showing at least five cards in the suit. Having seen dummy, you will be well-placed to judge whether to lead a second heart or to switch to a minor.

(b)
- ♠ K54
- ♥ A1074
- ♦ 6
- ♣ J10987

You could lead the ♥A again but this time you have two very attractive alternatives. The club sequence offers a very safe lead and might well be your choice if you didn't have something even better.

Lead your singleton diamond. With ♠K54, you will always make the ♠K if declarer holds the ace and now you can try to put partner in to give you a ruff. Whether that will mean leading a club, ace and another heart, or a daring underlead of the ♥A, will depend on what you see in dummy and the early play. Note that the ♠K, giving probable control of the trump suit, greatly improves the chance of success for the singleton lead.

(c)
♠ Q82
♥ Q97
♦ AJ875
♣ J7

This one is an easy heart lead. ♣J7 is quite dangerous and anyway you probably don't want a ruff this time as it rates to be made with your natural trump trick. A trump would obviously be foolish, while a diamond is also risky.

Having decided to lead partner's suit, the correct card is the ♥7. You will meet people who believe it correct to lead top of partner's bid suit from any holding. They are mistaken. Except in certain rare situations, it is best to lead low from an honor, just as you would in an unbid suit and for the same reasons.

5.

West	North	East	South
West	*North*	*East*	*South*
–	–	Pass	1♠
Pass	2♦	Pass	2♥
Pass	2NT	Pass	3♥
Pass	4♥	All Pass	

(a)   ♠ KJ83
        ♥ 1098
        ♦ J53
        ♣ A86

Declarer has shown at least 5-5 in the majors and will surely want to establish his spades by ruffing in dummy. Your priority must be to try to prevent his doing that in order to protect your own spade holding. Lead a trump, the ♥10, and hope to get in quickly to continue to play trumps.

(b)   ♠ KJ83
        ♥ J76
        ♦ J1062
        ♣ AK

Again, it is important to draw trumps to protect your spade holding but there is another priority here. Declarer has at most three minor suit cards and if he wins the opening lead may be able to discard a losing club on dummy's diamonds. Before playing trumps, lead a top club – the king from ace, king doubleton – and decide whether to cash a second round or switch to a trump when you see dummy and the play to trick one.

(c)   ♠ 975432
        ♥ A
        ♦ J106
        ♣ A85

Ace and another club could be the winning lead if partner holds the king, but there is another attractive line of defense. Your six small spades suggest that declarer will need to do very little work to establish his side-suit this time, but partner may be ruffing very quickly or, perhaps, over-ruffing dummy. Lead a spade, intending to continue spades when in with ♥A and, if partner can over-ruff, he can then put you back in with ♣A to lead a third spade.

6.	West	North	East	South
	Pass	Pass	Pass	1♥
	Pass	1NT	Pass	2♦
	Pass	2♥	All Pass	

(a)
- ♠ 764
- ♥ 853
- ♦ AJ105
- ♣ KQJ

The club sequence looks obvious, does it not? Yet the clubs will probably keep. Of more concern is protecting your diamond holding and the way to do that is to lead a trump to prevent ruffs in the dummy. Dummy can have no long suit on which declarer can pitch his club losers so you will get a chance later to take your clubs.

(b)
- ♠ 764
- ♥ 42
- ♦ AJ963
- ♣ QJ10

You have even better diamonds this time but, curiously, there is less reason to lead trumps. The reason is that partner probably has more trumps and less diamonds than in the previous example and will be sitting there happily looking forward to over-ruffing dummy. This time you do lead the obvious ♣Q, top of your sequence.

(c)
- ♠ 875
- ♥ Q4
- ♦ AJ104
- ♣ QJ97

Back to the original diamond holding, making it quite possible that dummy has two diamonds and three hearts and will be able to ruff fruitfully. You would like to lead trumps again but the queen doubleton lead will give away a trick far too often. Just lead ♣Q, top of your sequence, and hope that partner is either the one with the doubleton diamond or can get in quickly and switch to trumps.

conclusion

I hope that you have found this introduction to opening leads easy to understand and useful. If you have understood everything here you will be well equipped to make effective opening leads, though nobody can expect to find the right lead all the time. Like most things in bridge, you have to take a long-term view.

You should now appreciate the benefits of following a system of leads. In other words, of always leading the same card from similar holdings so as to help partner to understand what you have led from so that he can plan the most effective defense.

But following rules blindly is not what good bridge is about. You have been told not to lead a suit in which you hold an unsupported ace against a suit contract, yet have also seen examples where to do so was recommended. And you have heard that a solid sequence is a very good lead, yet have also seen examples where you would lead some other suit despite holding such a sequence. The message is to think flexibly, to bear in mind what you are trying to achieve. That, very simply, is to defeat your opponents' contract. Do not just look at your thirteen cards, listen to the clues contained in the bidding and you will be a better leader for it.

Good luck.